An Life cycles

FISH

by Honor Head

ticktock

KENSINGTON & CHELSEA
LIBRARIES SERVICE

Askews	
J571.817	
	PO-11050

Copyright © ticktock Entertainment Ltd 2007

First published in Great Britain in 2007 by ticktock Media Ltd,
2 Orchard Business Centre, North Farm Road, Tunbridge Wells, Kent, TN2 3XF

ticktock project editor: Ruth Owen
ticktock project designer: Sara Greasley
With thanks to: Trudi Webb, Sally Morgan and Elizabeth Wiggans

ISBN 978-1-84696-074-1 pbk

Printed in China

A CIP catalogue record for this book is available from the British Library.
No part of this publication may be reproduced, copied, stored in a retrieval system or transmitted in any form or by any means electronic, mechanical, photocopying, recording or otherwise without prior written permission of the copyright owner.

Picture credits (t=top; b=bottom; c=centre; l=left; r=right):
FLPA: 5b, 7t, 7b, 8 main, 11b, 12b, 16, 17, 20, 21, 25t, 27b, 28–29 main, 30c. Nature Picture Library: 15cr, 15cl.
NHPA: 14cl, 19b. Shutterstock: OFC, 1, 2, 3, 4tl, 4c, 5t, 6tl, 6b, 8tl, 9t, 9c, 9b, 10tl, 10 main, 11t, 12tl, 13t, 13b, 14tl, 14ct, 14cr, 14b, 15t, 15bl, 15br, 18 main, 19t, 22tl, 23, 24tl, 24b, 25b, 26, 27t, 28tl, 29b, 30tl, 31, OBC.
Superstock: 22c. ticktock image archive: map page 6, 18tl.

Every effort has been made to trace copyright holders, and we apologise in advance for any omissions. We would be pleased to insert the appropriate acknowledgments in any subsequent edition of this publication.

Contents

Words that look **bold like this** are in the glossary.

What is a fish?

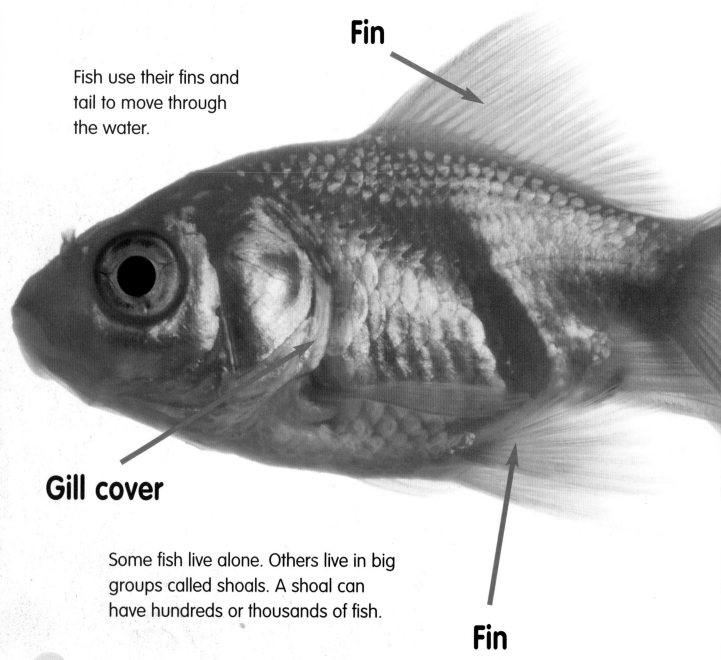

Fish are covered in scales that help to protect them.

A fish is an animal that lives in water. A fish usually has fins and **scales**. It can breathe underwater using body parts called **gills**. The gills take **oxygen** out of the water and pass it into the fish's body.

Fin

Fish use their fins and tail to move through the water.

Gill cover

Some fish live alone. Others live in big groups called shoals. A shoal can have hundreds or thousands of fish.

Fin

These fish eggs have been attached to an underwater rock by a female fish.

Most fish **reproduce** by laying eggs. The eggs are very small and soft. The female fish usually lays hundreds of eggs in one go.

Sharks are a type of fish. Some sharks, such as the great white shark, give birth to live babies called pups.

A great white shark.

Tail

AMAZING FISH FACT
When great white shark pups are born they are over a metre long and have sharp teeth, ready for hunting!

Fish habitats

Blue tang fish live in holes and cracks on coral reefs.

A habitat is the place where a plant or an animal lives. The ocean is a habitat, so are rivers and lakes. Many fish live in the ocean which is **saltwater**. Other types of fish live in **freshwater** ponds or streams.

Fish live in all the world's oceans.

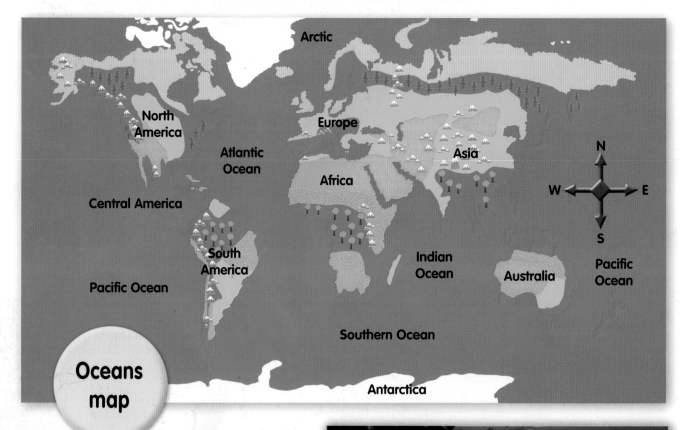

Arctic

North America

Europe

Atlantic Ocean

Asia

Africa

Central America

South America

Indian Ocean

Australia

Pacific Ocean

Pacific Ocean

N

W E

S

Southern Ocean

Oceans map

Antarctica

Some of the most colourful fish live around **coral reefs**. These reefs grow near to the surface of the water in warm oceans.

There are lots of coral reefs in the Pacific and Indian Oceans.

6

Some strange looking fish live at the very bottom of deep oceans where it is cold, dark and there is very little food.

The deepwater fangtooth fish has a huge mouth that helps it catch any fish it can find – even if the fish is the same size as the fangtooth fish!

AMAZING FISH FACT
The fangtooth fish has huge eyes to help it see in the dark.

The mudskipper is a fish that lives in shallow water in muddy freshwater **swamps**. It spends most of its time out of water and can 'walk' using its fins.

Fin

Ocean fish

Stonefish live on the ocean floor. They look just like stones and have a nasty sting!

Ocean fish can be just a few centimetres long, or enormous like the whale shark – the biggest fish in the world! Some ocean fish don't even look like fish, but more like seaweed or stones.

Whale shark

AMAZING FISH FACT
The whale shark can grow to 15 metres long. It's not a hunter though, it only eats **plankton**.

The leafy seadragon lives in warm oceans around Australia. It hides in seaweed using its leaf-like decorations as **camouflage**.

Many fish that live in coral reefs have bright colours or patterns that help keep them safe from **predators**, such as bigger fish.

This leafy seadragon is 45 centimetres long.

Pretend eye

This butterfly fish's black spot looks like an eye. A predator is not sure which end is the right end to attack.

Sea anemone

Tomato clownfish

The tomato clownfish lives on coral reefs hidden from predators among the stinging tentacles of **sea anemones**.

The clownfish's body is covered in a special slime. Scientists believe the slime protects the fish from the anemone's stings.

Freshwater fish

Some freshwater fish live in clear, flowing streams or rivers. Others live in ponds where the water is very still and where lots of weeds grow.

Perch live in rivers and lakes. Females lay 300,000 eggs at one time!

Catfish live in lakes and rivers. They eat fish, shellfish and any other small creatures they can find. They usually feed at night.

Barbel →

AMAZING FISH FACT
Catfish use their long whiskers, or barbels, to feel for food along the bottom of lakes and rivers.

Piranhas live in freshwater rivers in South America.

Piranhas are freshwater fish that eat other fish, insects, seeds and fruit. But sometimes piranhas will eat larger animals!

If the river dries up during a hot time of year, the piranhas are forced to live together in a small amount of water. If a large animal, such as a horse, steps into the water, the hungry piranhas will attack as a group!

Piranhas have razor-sharp teeth!

Mum meets dad

This is a pair of long-nosed butterfly fish. All butterfly fish pair for life.

Most fish reproduce every year. Some fish find a mate and stay together as a pair for life. Other fish have a new partner each year. Many fish **mate** with more than one partner in the same year.

Hammerhead sharks can live in shoals of over 500 sharks. The strongest female swims in the middle of the shoal.

When she is ready to mate, the strongest female starts shaking her head from side side. This makes the other females swim to the edges the shoal.

AMAZING FISH FACT

Sharks live in all the world's oceans. They have been around since before the dinosaurs!

Now the strongest female is the centre of attention and is sure to get a mate.

The angelfish pair in this photo are guarding their eggs.

Freshwater angelfish stay together as a pair for life. After mating, the female lays about 1,000 eggs on a leaf.

Eggs

A male emperor angelfish lives with up to five female mates. If the male dies, one of the females turns into a male fish and becomes the leader of the group!

Emperor angelfish live on coral reefs.

What is a life cycle?

A life cycle is all the different **stages** and changes that a plant or animal goes through in its life. The diagrams on these pages show examples of fish life cycles.

This is a pair of red flower horn fish. There are about 24,500 different types of fish.

1 A pair of lionfish

An adult male and female fish meet. Some fish make a nest.

FISH LIFE CYCLE
Many fish have a life cycle with these stages.

4 Baby salmon

2 Fertilised fish eggs

The female fish lays her eggs. The male fish covers the eggs with a liquid from his body called sperm. Now the eggs are fertilised.

Baby fish called fry hatch from the eggs. The tiny babies take care of themselves. They have a yolk sack which they use as food.

3 A pair of angelfish

Some fish guard their eggs. Others leave them to hatch on their own.

SHARK LIFE CYCLE
Some sharks have a life cycle with these stages.

1 A pair of nurse sharks

An adult male and female shark meet and mate.

2 A female lemon shark and pups

The female shark gives birth to lots of pups at the same time.

3 A black tip shark pup

As soon as they are born, the pups take care of themselves. They have teeth and are ready to hunt.

Amazing fish life cycles

Seahorse

Lionfish

In this book we are going to find out about some amazing life cycles – from tiny seahorses to colourful lionfish.

15

Deepsea anglerfish

Anglerfish live at the very bottom of deep oceans where it is very dark. The female has a long spine which comes out of her head. On the end is a ball that can glow like a light.

The female anglerfish can open her mouth really wide to eat fish the same size as her.

The female anglerfish uses her light to attract other fish – then she eats them!

Light

The male anglerfish cannot feed himself. As soon as he is old enough he has to find a female to live with.

The small male attaches himself to a female. They stay together for life. The male gets smaller and smaller.

Female

AMAZING FISH FACT

The male anglerfish becomes part of the female's body! When she eats, the food goes into the male's body, too.

Male

When it is time to reproduce and lay eggs, the female already has her mate with her.

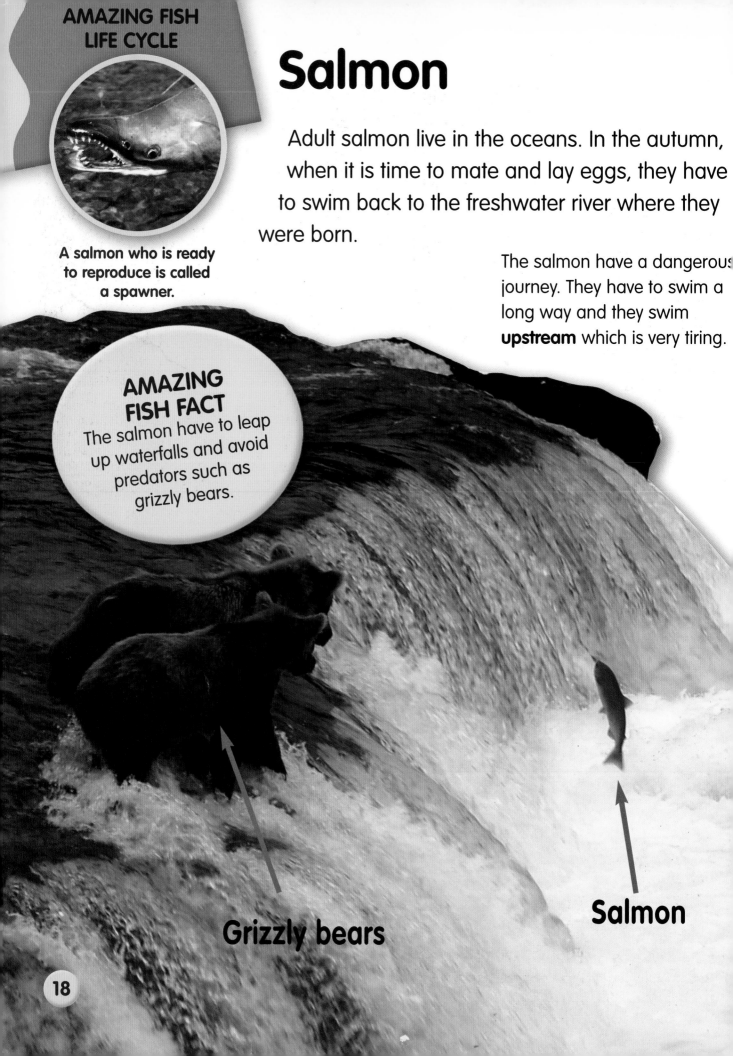

A salmon who is ready
to reproduce is called
a spawner.

Salmon

Adult salmon live in the oceans. In the autumn, when it is time to mate and lay eggs, they have to swim back to the freshwater river where they were born.

The salmon have a dangerous journey. They have to swim a long way and they swim **upstream** which is very tiring.

AMAZING FISH FACT
The salmon have to leap up waterfalls and avoid predators such as grizzly bears.

Grizzly bears

Salmon

When a female salmon reaches the spawning ground she makes four or five nests called redds. She lays about 1,000 eggs in each nest. Then a male fertilises the eggs.

Thousands of spawners gather in the same place.

The eggs hatch after four months. The small salmon are called alevins. They have an orange yolk sack which contains all the food they will need to grow.

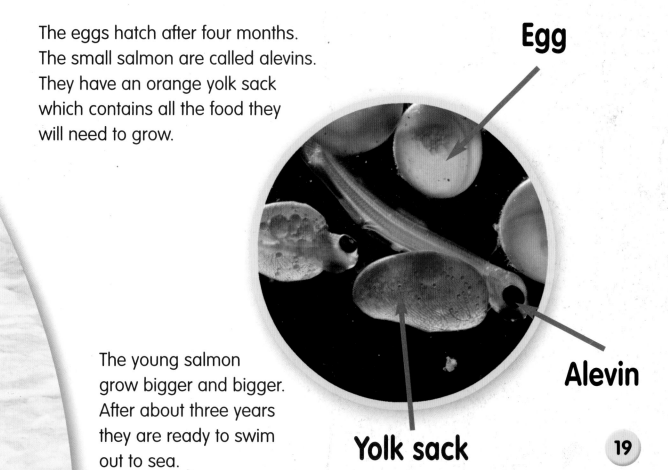

Egg

Alevin

Yolk sack

The young salmon grow bigger and bigger. After about three years they are ready to swim out to sea.

Stickleback

Sticklebacks are tiny fish – they grow to just five centimetres long. Some sticklebacks live in saltwater close to the coast. Others live in freshwater ponds, lakes and rivers.

Sticklebacks feed on tiny shellfish and the fry and eggs of other fish.

Nest

Between March and August the male stickleback changes colour to attract a mate.

Then the male stickleback builds a nest from bits of plant. He does a zigzag dance in front of the nest to attract a female.

During the mating season, the underside of the male's body becomes a bright orange-red colour, his eyes turn blue and silver scales appear on his back.

Lots of different females lay their eggs in the male's nest. Then he fertilises them.

AMAZING FISH FACT
The male stickleback guards the eggs in his nest and looks after the young when they hatch.

Male

Female

21

Sharks have a skeleton made of cartilage. This is the bendy stuff your ears are made of.

Dogfish

Dogfish live in the ocean. They are a type of small shark. Adult dogfish are about one metre long. They spend most of their time on the seabed hunting for crabs, prawns and small fish.

After mating, the female dogfish lays her eggs. Each egg is in its own little leathery case.

This is a pair of lesser spotted dogfish.

The female attaches the egg cases to pieces of seaweed so that they do not float away and get lost or damaged. The baby dogfish growing inside the case is called an embryo.

The embryo will stay in the case for about nine months. As it grows it curls around the inside of its egg case.

The egg cases are full of food for the embryo to eat.

By the time the baby dogfish is ready to hatch it will be about 10 centimetres long – twice as long as its egg case.

AMAZING FISH FACT

Empty dogfish egg cases are sometimes washed up onto beaches. People call them mermaids' purses.

Embryo

Egg case

Seahorse

This very unusual looking fish has a horse-like head and a tail it can use to hold onto things. The seahorse can move each of its eyes separately – one can look forwards while the other looks backwards.

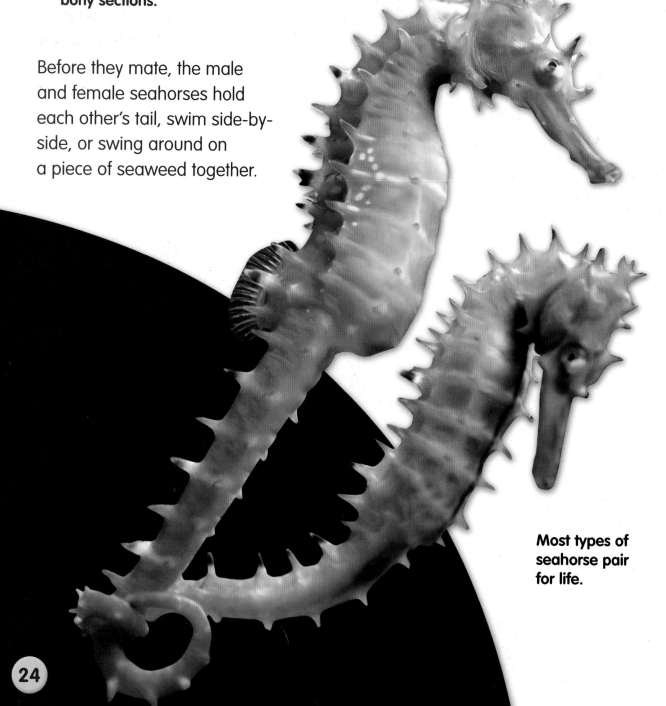

The seahorse's body is covered in armour made of hard, bony sections.

Before they mate, the male and female seahorses hold each other's tail, swim side-by-side, or swing around on a piece of seaweed together.

Most types of seahorse pair for life.

The male seahorse has a pouch on his tummy. The pouch is a bit like a pocket. The female lays her eggs inside the pouch and the male seahorse carries the eggs.

When the babies hatch, the male gives birth. He holds onto a piece of seaweed with his long tail. He rocks backwards and forwards until the babies pop out of his pouch. This can last for about two days.

Baby seahorse **Pouch**

AMAZING FISH FACT
Seahorses can change colour to match their surroundings.

Lionfish live on coral
reefs in warm seas.

Lionfish

Adult lionfish usually live alone, but when they are ready to mate they get together in groups. For three or four days each male will try to get a female to notice him.

Sometimes the males will fight.
They bite each other and ram
each other with their spiky fins.

**AMAZING
FISH FACT**
The lionfish's needle-like fins
can give a predator a
poisonous sting.

Fins

Adult lionfish are about 30 centimetres long.

When the male has found a partner, the two fish swim face to face and turn around in circles. They dance to the surface of the water.

On the surface of the water the female lays a ball of thousands of eggs. When the male has fertilised the eggs, the parents leave. After about three months the eggs hatch.

Baby lionfish

After hatching, the baby lionfish sink to the seabed to hide away from predators, such as bigger fish.

An adult hammerhead
is about three to four
metres long.

Hammerhead shark

Hammerhead sharks live in warm parts of
the Pacific, Indian and Atlantic Oceans.
They are strong swimmers and have
been known to attack people!

Dorsal fin

The hammerhead
shark has eyes and
ears at each end of its
wide head. Scientists
believe having eyes like
this might help the
shark to see all around
it when it is hunting.

Gill slits

The female hammerhead shark gives birth to about 20 to 40 pups at a time.

The pups are about 70 centimetres long when they are born. They look like small versions of the adults. The pups have to look after themselves as soon as they are born.

Eye

Hammerhead sharks eat fish and other sharks. Stingrays are their favourite food.

AMAZING FISH FACT

Some sharks have several rows of very sharp teeth. When a tooth falls out, one from the row behind pushes forward to take its place.

Stingray

That's amazing!

Many of the pictures in this book were taken using a special underwater camera.

All fish big or small use their gills to breathe underwater. If humans want to spend time underwater studying fish life cycles and photographing them we have to wear diving suits and breathe oxygen from a tank.

AMAZING FISH FACT

The sunfish can grow to nearly four metres long, and can weigh up to 2,250 kilograms.

Sunfish

A female sunfish can lay 300 million eggs each year. Each egg is smaller than a fullstop.

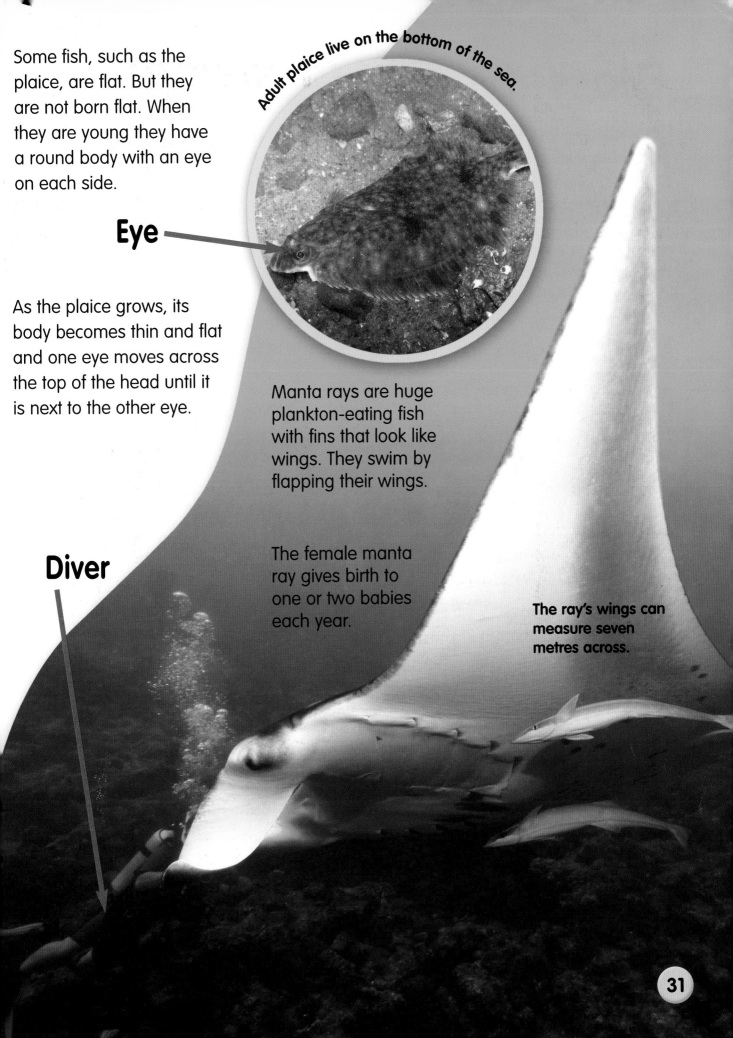

Some fish, such as the plaice, are flat. But they are not born flat. When they are young they have a round body with an eye on each side.

Eye

As the plaice grows, its body becomes thin and flat and one eye moves across the top of the head until it is next to the other eye.

Manta rays are huge plankton-eating fish with fins that look like wings. They swim by flapping their wings.

Diver

The female manta ray gives birth to one or two babies each year.

The ray's wings can measure seven metres across.

Glossary

camouflage – Colours, marks or a shape that hides an animal from its predators, and the animals it hunts.

coral reefs – Underwater places that look rocky but are actually made from the bodies of coral animals called polyps. The polyps have hard skeletons that join together. When a polyp dies, its skeleton stays as part of the reef, so the reefs gets bigger and bigger.

freshwater – Rainwater, and the water in ponds and some rivers. It is not salty.

gills – Breathing organs (parts of the body) in animals that live in water.

mate – When a male and female animal meet and have babies.

oxygen – A gas that all animals need for life.

plankton – Tiny animals and plants that live in oceans and lakes. They are so small you need a microscope to see them.

predators – Animals which hunt and kill other animals for food.

reproduce – To have babies.

saltwater – Water with salt in it. The oceans and some lakes are saltwater.

scales – Small, overlapping sections of hard skin that cover the bodies of fish.

sea anemones – An ocean animal with stinging tentacles – it looks like a plant!

stages – Different times of an animal's life when the animal changes.

swamps – Very wet areas with lots of water plants.

upstream – The opposite direction to the flow of water in a river or stream.

Index